D0965458

A   GIFT   FOR

_____

F R O M

_____

*A Love That Won't Walk Away*

KATHY TROCCOLI

Nashville, Tennessee

Copyright © 2005 by Kathy Troccoli

Published by the J. Countryman® division of the Thomas Nelson Book Group,
Nashville, Tennessee 37214

All rights reserved. No portion of this publication may be reproduced, stored in a
retrieval system or transmitted in any form by any means—electronic, mechanical,
photocopying, recording, or any other—except for brief quotations in printed reviews,
without the prior written permission of the publisher.

Scriptures with the notation:
    (NKJV) are from the *New King James Version*® of the Bible.
        ©1979, 1980, 1982, 1992, Thomas Nelson, Inc., Publisher. All rights reserved.
    (NCV) are from the *New Century Version*® of the Bible.
        © 1987, 1988, 1991 by Thomas Nelson, Inc. All rights reserved.
    (NIV) are from the *New International Version* of the Bible.
        © 1984 by the International Bible Society.
        Used by permission of Zondervan Bible Publishers.
    (NRSV) are from the *New Revised Standard Version* of the Bible.
        © 1989 by the Division of Christian Education of the National Council
        of the Churches of Christ in the USA. Used by permission.
    (NLT) are from *The Holy Bible, New Living Translation*.
        © 1996. Used by permission of Tyndale House Publishers, Inc.,
        Wheaton, Illinois. All rights reserved.

Project Editor: Kathy Baker

Designed by Koechel Peterson & Associates, Minneapolis, Minnesota

ISBN 1-4041-0213-2

Printed and bound in the United States of America

CONTENTS

"The LORD your God

will go with you.

He will not leave you or forget you."

DEUTERONOMY 31:6 NCV

SHE WAS ECSTATIC. Here she was at a little bed and breakfast with the man she had exchanged vows with twenty-five years before. They had just finished a romantic, candlelit dinner. He had amazed her because he had actually called the restaurant and requested a special table by the fire. She looked out the window to see a wintry scene that was right out of Currier & Ives.

They reminisced about times past and the amazing children they had raised. It was a different season now, with those kids out of the house. What was going to be the new goal? Where should they be five years from now? She always enjoyed talks like this with him, because it felt like they were truly connecting. He had been a little distant lately, and she had begun to worry. But tonight brought her a new sense of love for him and a great sense of relief.

The experience at the restaurant ended in such a fabulous way. They even lingered over coffee. After a pleasant ride home and a wonderful night in every respect, she went to bed with a peace in her heart and new dreams for the future.

One month later . . .

Although things had not continued quite as beautifully as that night in the restaurant, she still possessed a peace about the future. He was being distant again and had been on the computer much more than usual, but Christmas was just around the corner. She could already feel the joy of the whole family being together again.

The garage door opened and he walked into the house. Her life was about to be changed forever. He was agitated and she didn't know why. The keys were thrown, the tie was ripped off, and he headed straight for the bedroom. *He must have had a really bad day at work.* This was different, though. Something definitely felt wrong. She wasn't even sure she wanted to ask him about it. Mustering her courage, she forced herself to follow him to the bedroom.

"What in the world is going on?"

He seemed to sense the weight of her question and barely looked at her when he revealed that he was no longer in love with her and wanted to leave. It felt weird and surreal. Was this coming out of the mouth of *her* husband? This happened to other people. Did he really just say that?

". . . Because I deserve to be happy."

He what? The story was gradually revealed. Through a fluke, he had been in contact with his high school sweetheart over the Internet. He'd been reminded of the young innocent love that the two of them had shared. He ached to be that happy again. He was convinced that this other woman could provide that happiness. He wanted out.

He left the next day.

Julie and Beth were carrying packages through the mall for the umpteenth time since becoming best friends three years before. Their motto was simple: there was always room in the closet for one more pair of shoes. Shopping together was not just a way to pass the time; it was an emotional experience. They could just look at each other and laugh. Currently, they both had tears flowing down their faces as they reminisced about past adventures.

"They probably don't have these stores in Phoenix." It slipped out of Beth's mouth.

"In Phoenix? What are you talking about?" Julie suddenly realized that Beth had stopped smiling.

"Oh, Julie. My boss called me in today. My position is being transferred to the Phoenix office. If I want to keep my job, I'm going to have to move. I've already put in eight years with the company. I can't just throw that out. I've been trying to sift through this all day. I was going to tell you at dinner."

Three weeks later, Beth was two thousand miles away, and Julie was walking alone through the same mall. The last thing she wanted to do was to ever buy another pair of shoes.

Know that the LORD your God is God,

the faithful God.

He will keep his agreement of love

for a thousand lifetimes

for people who love him

and obey his commands.

DEUTERONOMY 7:9 NCV

A LOVE THAT WON'T WALK AWAY

Some days are easier than others 'cause life's not eas
Some days you hide under the covers till the storm clouds b
You feel like your faith is dying, but please don't gi

'Cause that's just how it goes how life turns, how it rolls, through the fire and through
It may hurt, it may bruise, it may leave you confused, but you wil
'cause His kind of love is a love that won't wa

So don't let the rain take your
Don't let the wind beat y
Don't let the waves crash against you and turn your hear
'cause God is right there beside you and He wants you

Oh, that's just ho
How life turns, how it rolls, through the fire and through
It may hurt, it may bruise, it may leave you confused, but you will
'cause His kind of love is a love that won't wa

16

OUR TENDENCY
*to Leave and Be Left*

## A Love That Won't Walk Away

BY JESS CATES / TY LACY

Some days are easier than others
'cause life's not tailor made.
Some days you hide under the covers
till the storm clouds blow away.
You feel like your faith is dying,
but please don't give up yet.

'Cause that's just how it goes
How life turns, how it rolls,
Through the fire and through the pain.
It may hurt, it may bruise,
It may leave you confused,
but you will be okay
'cause His kind of love is a love
that won't walk away.

So don't let the rain take your courage.
Don't let the wind beat you down.
Don't let the waves crash against you
and turn your heart around,
'cause God is right there beside you
and He wants you to know…

Oh, that's just how it goes.
How life turns, how it rolls,
Through the fire and through the pain.
It may hurt, it may bruise,
It may leave you confused,
but you will be okay
'cause His kind of love is a love
that won't walk away.

I've been singing the lyrics of that song for the past couple of years. Its message challenges me every time I hear the words. We all ask a similar question: is the comfort that the song implies real? Can I truly get lasting peace from a supernatural presence, and will it *really* last? That's the honest question.

Even the title is incredibly intriguing . . .

*A Love That Won't Walk Away*

I have "lost" many people. My beloved parents, some close relatives, and some dear friends. As I continue to have conversations with women from all walks of life I realize that many of us share a common "hurt." It is the deep pain in our souls that can loom over us for years like a dark stormy cloud.

# NONE OF US
*wants to be "left."*

And yet we all are left at some point in our lives. I wish it weren't true. Someone leaves—whether through a deliberate act of walking out the door or the devastating passage of death—it happens. It is a part of living here and enduring mortal bodies and possessing selfish hearts.

We were all built for relationship—first and foremost with our Creator, who in turn blessed us with the desire for relationship. There is a yearning in all of us to love and be loved. There is a longing to know and be known.

If we should be so blessed as to find a special relationship in this life, we certainly don't want to lose it. Some of us may cling too tightly, and some may take it for granted. But truth be told, none of us wants it to change. Not one of us wants to lose someone we love. The relationship is safety. It is comfort. It brings stability and a sense of well-being. We belong.

I first heard the song "A Love That Won't Walk Away" on a demo tape when I was looking for new music for an upcoming CD. I've written many songs, but I am always looking for the "gold nuggets" out there in the world of music. I look for those treasures that I could "own" for myself, and most of all be able to "give away" to others. I yearn for people to know the riches of God's love.

From the minute I heard . . .

> *Life's not tailor made . . .*

To . . .

> *Some days you hide under the covers . . .*

It was like I was screaming inside. This was way more than just a song . . . I thought, "That's me!" That *is* me . . . I knew if people heard this they would feel the same way.

*Am I going to make it?*

*How could this happen?*

*I don't deserve it.*

*How could there be a God*

*Who would allow this?"*


Such words have echoed

  Through the chambers

    Of Heaven millions of times . . .


Because I have been through my own "dark nights of
the soul," and because I have seen the "joy come in the
morning," I *must* sing about His love.

When I sing . . .

*But you will be okay . . .*

I see the arrow of God's hope pierce through the most despairing heart. Don't we all need to be reminded?

As a matter of fact, I could never sing about it enough. I pray I will sing it far into eternity.

I could never speak about it enough. I will be talking about it through forever.

I could never think about it enough. It will still occupy my mind thousands and thousands of years from now.

I could never stop giving it.

Sometimes you may know someone who will do something that is contrary to what you have experienced from them. You might say . . .

*That was so out of character for him.*

We can never say that about Jesus. He is consistent and unconditional in his wisdom and his love. You can count on it. He is the house you come home to after along trip. It's safe and secure. It's a haven and a hiding place. That is so reassuring to me. It brings me such comfort, especially being single and now without parents.

He understands.
>He doesn't blame us.
>He doesn't hold anything against us.

He's honest.
>He sees our hearts
>And knows our deepest feelings.

Nothing is shocking to God.
>A God acquainted with sorrows.
>He waits patiently—
>for our surrender.

He's got a bigger and broader view.
>A profound and great knowing
>That all is well

And that all will be well
>In his hands.

The keys to every door
>Are in his hands.
>Our future is so safe with him.

I had very little relationship with Jesus when my father died. It was all so confusing to me. I remember one particular day pretty vividly. An ambulance waited at the end of our driveway. I watched as my father ever so slowly walked toward the vehicle. He stopped and turned around to the house that he cherished and said, "I'm leaving all this . . ." he *was* leaving, knowing that he would never return. My uncle then took the arm of this ashen, frail, and tired man and helped him walk the rest of the way. He had fought a good fight. He knew it was almost over. I was too young to really know the deep agony my dad must have felt as he left his home. I remember the pain in my heart as I saw him take a teary last look at the place he worked so hard to give to my mom and sister and me.

Today I think of the last words I heard my father speak as he said goodbye to everything he loved in life.

*"I'm leaving all this."*

There is great pain in being left, but there is also deep pain in the leaving. I will never forget that scene as long as I live. I also remember many years later when my mother said to my sister and me . . .

*"I don't want to leave you. I want to know you will be all right. I want to see my grandchildren grow."*

Today I am certain of the life that my parents have been given. I often say that with Jesus we go from "life to life." I am also certain that we will all be reunited some day. The "leaving" will be just for a moment on God's timetable. I know that it is just "goodbye for now." Because of the resurrection we can experience love that will never walk away.

The world lost a life—
Your heart lost a love.

A face you can't see
A voice you can't hear
A hand you can't hold.

Memories.

Some fade

Some stay—
As clear and bright
As a beautiful summer sun.

They visit us—
They comfort us
Until the day we are reunited.
Sheer joy.
What a day that will be . . .

A few years ago, Tom Hanks starred in the movie *Castaway*. I am a big fan of his, and I was intrigued by the fact that he would be the only actor on the screen during most of the movie. He played a survivor of a plane crash who was stranded on an island for several years before he was rescued. It is so hard to imagine being alone for that long—let alone protecting yourself from the elements and being responsible for the food and water that your body would require. An especially interesting part of the film was the "companion" that he cherished during his time on the island. Soon after the crash some debris washed up on the beach. Amidst the rubble was a volleyball. It was painfully clear how lonely the castaway was to not only try to keep himself alive, but not have human contact. Day after long day he was without conversation. There was no hand to hold and no voice to hear. The castaway eventually drew a face on the volleyball and "Wilson" was born. Wilson listened even if it was just so the lonely man could hear the sound of his own voice. He would often keep the "face" of Wilson in eye view. Wilson was a friend and a comforter.

Most of us will never be stranded on an island. We will never know that kind of desertion and "aloneness." But many of us have felt that alone and deserted. We have similar stories of being left on the "desert island."

"The Lord your God
will go with you.
He will not leave you
or forget you."

DEUTERONOMY 31:6 NCV

## ABANDONED.

As I continue to grow with Jesus I am so aware of how my emotions have gotten in the way of his truth. He gave his life so that I could have life. He sent a comforter so that I would be comforted. He rose from the dead so that I could have eternal life. That life starts now and not in forever. *Today* is the day that the Lord has made. Resurrection life and power can lift me above my emotions and my circumstances to the truth of the promises of God. When I cry out the Lord always hears, and he loves me beyond measure.

In my own years of my deepest depression, I felt lost and abandoned. There was a sense of utter hopelessness. I needed the help of friends, doctors, and Almighty God to clear the fog. When the fog did clear, I was able to truly

not only hear the promises but cling to them. Bank on them amid the storms. The weight was off my back, and I could grab hold of the love that hadn't left. Did you catch that? Grab hold of the love *that hadn't left*. And when I grab hold of him, I am taken to higher places.

Sometimes we are in so much pain that we walk farther into the wilderness. We get cold and hungry and weak. We lose our way. We may hear voices of family and friends calling our names, but they seem far in the distance. What we must continue to realize that this life will be disappointing. It will have heartache. We will not be loved in ways that we had hoped to be loved. And you know what? We also will be guilty of failing others in the same way. And many times we will march ourselves right out there into the wilderness. We feel abandoned, so we go to places that will make us even feel lonelier. It is not in our nature to have our first response be . . . .

> *God, I need you.*
>
> *You have loved me well.*
>
> *. . . Continue, Lord Jesus.*

*We will lie on the sand and talk to Wilson before we ever pour our hearts out — to the lover of our souls.*

I am not saying that we should just "buck up." There are times to sob into our pillows. There are times to yell and scream and get it out. We must remember, though, that he is right there in the midst of our despair.

God's love is like nothing we have ever known.

God answered the call of hate to stay right there on the cross.

The agony.
   The darkness.
   "Come down...
         if you're God."
   They taunted.
   They mocked.

"Surely you can come down."

Others tenderly whispered
      As their tears fell...
      "You can come down—
      Can't you, Lord?
            You are God.

There was arrogance

Beneath the cross,
      And
      There was humility
            Beneath the cross.

But the same question was asked,
"If you are God come down."
      Certainly he could,
            But he would not.

There was a perfect plan
      And an ultimate purpose.
And three days later—
      there was a resurrection.

It changed eternity
      for all of humanity.

"If you're God..."
      —We continue to ask
      Two thousand years later.

He continues to say...
      "I love you so...
      Be still
            and know that I am."

He yearned for us to know that love in our lifetime—truly know the love that stayed there in the pain on the cross and that would stay there through our pain today.

When we are bleeding we must fall at his feet and let the healing balm in his hand touch our desperate bodies and souls. It is much easier to lie there and die—or so we think. When we turn our backs on his love we also turn our backs on his plans for our lives. The dreams he has for our lives. The joy, hope, and peace that await us.

That is why the scriptures say that . . .

*Weeping may endure for the night . . .*

*But joy comes in the morning.*

PSALM 30:5 NKJV

When it is dark, it is so dark. When it is black, we forget there is any other color. When we feel pain, the ache occupies so much of our hearts there is barely room for anything else. He knows that. No day was darker than the day he hung on a cross. But no day was more hopeful than when he rose three days later.

The tomorrows come. And because he lives you can be awakened by a kiss of love. He never stops offering it to us and never withdraws it. You can open the curtains to hope and to life.

I remember the day when I was told that my mom had a limited time to live. I was alone in the hospital, but more than that I was feeling the deep sadness of being alone in the world. Surely God wasn't going to take my mother too . . .

*I have no husband and no children. I will be orphaned . . .*

I remembered his words . . .

*I will never fail you or forsake you.*

*I will always be with you.*

*I will never leave you.*

The words I knew from the scriptures. His promises—deliberate and clear. They raced through my mind.

*Is it true, Lord?*

*I mean—really true?*

*Will you stay with me?*

It is the cry of all of our hearts. It seems it happens from the minute we breathe our first breath. From the time we could cling, we cling. Did you ever see a baby cry desperately to be put back in its mother's or father's arms? Somehow the desperation stays with us.

*Don't leave.*

Knowing Jesus has absolutely given me a confidence to say . . .

*I will never be left.*

Will I feel lonely some days?

Do I live with an ache for my real home?

Yes. It is true for all of us.

But knowing Jesus makes all the difference. I often wonder how people go through this life without him. It makes me understand why so many of us turn to addictions and affairs and hopelessness and heartache. We are yearning for that "constant." It is because we weren't meant to live without him. He offers himself lavishly to us in all sorts of ways, yet we'll live in poverty when the riches of his love are there for the taking every minute of the day.

*For God so loved the world that he gave his only Son …*

JOHN 3:16 NLT

God loved and gave. He loves and gives. It wasn't just the one act on the cross. It is consistent and unwavering. It gives and gives and gives some more. The cross was just the beginning …

We see and understand so poorly. That's why his love seems so outrageous. It is so contrary to human love. He has a plan, and it is all based on his love for you and me. Somehow we believe he will walk out or "not make good" on his promises. Nothing is farther from the truth.

*The LORD is righteous in all his ways*
*And loving toward all he has made.*

PSALM 145:17 NIV

He is faithful to all his promises—not just some of his promises. Our experiences tell that promises will be broken. The most heart-wrenching of all are the promises of love. People can easily stop giving. They run out and they run dry. No more "best foot forward." No more honeymoon time. No more forever. It could be in marriage or with a close family member or a dear friend. It happens. The rug is pulled out from beneath us. We fall and feel like we will never get up again.

I remember when I first read the words of Jesus trying to simply communicate to the disciples the powerful gift that they were going to receive when he left them physically on earth. In John 14:16-19 he promised . . .

*But I will send you a comforter . . .*

*the spirit of truth . . .*

Right after that he said...

*I will not leave you as orphans ...*

Then he said...

*Because I live you also will live ...*

At those times in my life, when we feel abandoned... when we feel lost and left...even when we may want to die ...

His words are the same.

*You can live because I live.*

*You can go on because I will carry you and put you back down when you are stronger.*

"THE MOUNTAINS MAY DISAPPEAR,

AND THE HILLS MAY COME

TO AN END,

BUT MY LOVE WILL NEVER DISAPPEAR;

MY PROMISE OF PEACE

WILL NOT COME TO AN END,"

SAYS THE LORD

WHO SHOWS MERCY TO YOU."

ISAIAH 54:10 NCV

Jesus is more human, more loving, and more tenderhearted than the most sensitive of us.

One day, he sat in the temple with his followers observing the people as they walked by and dropped coins into the treasury.

The curious apostles would look, guess at the amount put in—and then comment on it.

"That's so-and-so, and that's that other fellow..."

Our Lord suddenly asked, "Who do you think gave most?"

Naturally, they tried to remember whose
money had made the loudest clank, and
Jesus had to start explaining everything,
educating them over and over again.

"Didn't you notice that women back there? No,
you didn't read her face; you didn't see that she
put in everything she had to her name.
In fact I tell you . . ."

And the apostles found out that they "hadn't
really seen anything, that they were blind,
dull and dense even in their curiosity.

Only our Lord had loved that woman and,
because he had, he'd seen and understood
and guessed.

He always looked with sympathy on everyone's
trial and sufferings, on his most secret
afflictions and most shameful grief.

The familiar story of the woman and her coin. I could just imagine how faceless and ordinary she was to everyone that day. She could have never imagined that the God of all riches not only saw her offering but also saw her heart. He knew the true state of affairs of her life. Jesus not only noticed—he knew—and was so pleased. I believe it moved him deeply and with great compassion to mention it to the disciples.

Appearances never fool God. I love that. When we can't see—he sees so clearly. He understands and looks with great sympathy on our earthly condition and our painful circumstances.

Two thousand years ago love appeared in the flesh. Love stayed with us awhile, and then love died so that we could live. Love rose again so that we would live forever. Love sent his spirit so that we would know that he would never leave.

I will never be left. You will never be left. Not by him. Never by him.

"MY SPIRIT AND MY WORDS THAT I GIVE YOU

WILL NEVER LEAVE YOU

OR YOUR CHILDREN

OR YOUR GRANDCHILDREN,

NOW AND FOREVER."

ISAIAH 59:21 NCV

LOVE STAYS.
   You wake up in the morning—
         and your whole world changes.
               Nothing will ever be
               as you have known it to be.

      The Lord is such
         A gentle shepherd
               A caring and dependable guide—
         He will not leave us broken
               He will not leave us lost

      He will not leave us . . .
      The only thing in life
      That I have learned never changes—
               Is the love of God.

      Yesterday
               Today
                     And forever

         It remains the same.

He said that he would never disappoint me.

 *He hasn't.*

He said that he would walk me through everything.

 *He has.*

He said that he would never leave me.

 *He hasn't and I know he never will.* ❋

## PSALM 34 NIV

I will extol the LORD at all times;
his praise will always be on my lips.
My soul will boast in the LORD;
let the afflicted hear and rejoice.
Glorify the LORD with me;
let us exalt his name together.

I sought the LORD, and he answered me;
he delivered me from all my fears.
Those who look to him are radiant;
their faces are never covered with shame.
This poor man called, and the LORD heard him;
he saved him out of all his troubles.
The angel of the LORD encamps
    around those who fear him,
and he delivers them.

Taste and see that the LORD is good;
blessed is the man who takes refuge in him.
Fear the LORD, you his saints,
or those who fear him lack nothing.
The lions may grow weak and hungry,
but those who seek the LORD lack no good thing.

KATHY TROCCOLI

Come, my children, listen to me;
I will teach you the fear of the LORD.
Whoever of you loves life
and desires to see many good days,
keep your tongue from evil
and your lips from speaking lies.
Turn from evil and do good;
seek peace and pursue it.

The eyes of the LORD are on the righteous
and his ears are attentive to their cry;
the face of the LORD is against those who do evil,
to cut off the memory of them from the earth.

The righteous cry out, and the LORD hears them;
he delivers them from all their troubles.
The LORD is close to the brokenhearted
and saves those who are crushed in spirit.

A righteous man may have many troubles,
but the LORD delivers him from them all;
he protects all his bones,
not one of them will be broken.

Evil will slay the wicked;
the foes of the righteous will be condemned.
The LORD redeems his servants;
no one will be condemned who takes refuge in him.

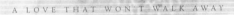

## A LOVE THAT WON'T WALK AWAY

Some days are easier than others 'cause life's not ea...
Some days you hide under the covers till the storm clouds ...
You feel like your faith is dying, but please don't go...

'Cause that's just how it goes how life turns, how it rolls, through the fire and through...
It may hurt, it may bruise, it may leave you confused, but you we...
'cause His kind of love is a love that won't ...

So don't let the rain take you...
Don't let the wind beat...
Don't let the waves crash against you and turn your hea...
'cause God is right there beside you and He wants you...

Oh, that's just h...
How life turns, how it rolls, through the fire and through...
It may hurt, it may bruise, it may leave you confused, but you wi...
'cause His kind of love is a love that won't ...

50

# GOD'S TENDENCY
*to Come and to Stay*

ONE OF MY FAVORITE movies is *The Goodbye Girl*. I've watched it several times over the years. It is extremely romantic and endearingly funny. It is also one of those films that has a fairytale ending and leaves you with a warm fuzzy feeling. Yes... that's why I love it and yes, that is what every woman longs for.

The original motion picture was made in the 1970s. It starred Richard Dreyfus and Marsha Mason. Their chemistry was so sweet, and the dialogue between them so brilliantly written by Neil Simon. I will sometimes refer to their conversations in many of my own.

To summarize the story, Marsha Mason's character comes home one day to find a Dear John letter from her boyfriend. She is devastated and tired of being "left," but she goes on to make a life for herself and her little daughter. Enter Richard Dreyfus. He plays a struggling, talented actor who is witty and soft hearted. As any great love story goes, he woos her, and her heart begins to soften. A trust is built again. Soon he gets an offer to play a big part. He must leave. You can imagine the rest. Her heart can't help but think . . .

*Here it is. It was just a matter of time. He is really going to leave.*

He deeply loves her and her daughter. You know that he is coming back and will be truly committed to the two of them. But she has trouble believing it. All she has known is "being left." She is the ultimate "goodbye girl." Teary and insecure she watches him leave. In this closing scene, he is catching a cab. Before he climbs into the taxi she opens a window facing the street. His beloved guitar is with her. It is a simple thing—but she finally "gets it" . . .

He is coming back!

Unfortunately many of us don't get to live in the fairy-tale. Oh, how we yearn for it! Our spirits still long for the lost Garden of Eden. But ultimately, through his grace, we will go from what I like to call "life to life" as our happy ending goes on for all eternity.

*Sometimes I think he created the sun to rise so that we would remember. With every sunrise and sunset there is the reminder that yesterday is gone and today starts anew. We can be ruled by our emotions. They are staring at us at the beginning of each day like dogs waiting to be let outside—scurrying around in a frenzy until their voices are heard. Emotions are real and they need to be addressed. But you are in charge of them. Especially as women, we can sit amid them like a pile of dirty laundry. Before we know it we are having a big old pity party right there with the dirty socks. We'll sit there for hours and even days. I know because I have done it.*

Read the scriptures about the days after the cruci-fixion. Can you imagine how abandoned the disciples felt? And what about Mary?

*Then the followers went back home. But Mary stood outside the tomb, crying. As she was crying, she bent down and looked inside the tomb. She saw two angels dressed in white, sitting where Jesus' body had been, one at the head and one at the feet.*

JOHN 20:10-12 NCV

Everyone left. Mary was at the tomb alone and she was crying. But as she was crying she bent over to look into the tomb. That is so significant. We can feel heartache and abandonment. He doesn't despise our tears. He tenderly hears them. But he wants us to *do* something. He wants us to bend over and look into the tomb. Just like Mary. Why? It is to see the resurrected Christ. The hope. The glory. The promises. It will all be there.

Satan wants us to never even get near it, let alone take a peek in. Why? Because he wants us to stay in the muck and mire of our fears, depression, and abandonment. It is so important to wake up every day with a mindset of "choosing life." Every single day there is a clear path before you. God has set it up that way.

The LORD's love never ends;

his mercies never stop.

They are new every morning;

LORD, your loyalty is great.

LAMENTATIONS 3:22, 23 NCV

He paves new paths that hold endless possibilities. He offers a clean slate.

*I'm alone...*
*No one understands...*

I continue to learn to get up and sort it all through. We need to turn on the lights because usually we are sulking in the dark. We need to live in the light of the truth of God. That's when you can truly see what needs to be kept and what needs to be thrown out.

*You aren't alone...*
*And he does understand.*

We often "speak" the absolute worst to ourselves and then wonder why our hearts are so heavy. We must blow wind back into the sails of our souls with the promises of God. They are all true, all rock-solid. Our emotions? They waver. That is why it is so important to "look into the tomb" every day. That is where you see impossible things becoming possible. The stone rolls away. That is where joy overcomes sorrow, because life emerges from death. That is where hope waits like a royal chariot to ride you into the riches of his plan for your life.

Let's go back to Mary at the tomb in John 20:13-16 (NCV). The angels asked her…

*"Woman, why are you crying?"*

She said…

*"They have taken away my Lord, and I don't know where they have put him."*

The scriptures then say that she turned around and saw Jesus standing there but didn't realize that it was him.

*"Woman,"* he said, *"Why are you crying? Whom are you are looking for?"*

*Thinking he was the gardener, she said to him, "Did you take him away, sir? Tell me where you put him, and I will get him."*

It gives me the chills when I read the next sentence …

*Jesus said to her, "Mary."*

She stopped. She realized who was speaking her name. Both the angels and Jesus asked her the same question. *Why are you crying?*

God never neglects our tears. I believe he is deeply moved by every one that falls. He knows our humanity, and he knows that life can hurt so badly down here.

Isn't it interesting that Mary did not realize that Jesus was right there? Isn't it true for us as well when we are in the midst of our pain? I believe that is why Jesus asked her who she was looking for. He knew the answer before she asked it. He knew that it had to be himself to meet the deepest cries of her heart.

In our pain and suffering, who and what are we looking for? Is it alcohol? Is it food? Is it sex? Is it drugs? Or is it just plain busyness? Many women especially search for comfort in what I like to call "frenetic church work." We are involved with endless spiritual activities that only serve to keep us away from God. *I don't want to feel! I don't want to hurt! Numb it. Kill it. Fill it.* We must do something. And all the while the One who truly satisfies and heals our hurting souls waits by our side.

And then Jesus did something so tender. He turned to Mary and called her by name. Oh, how he does the same for us in our heartache. He's there in the stillness. Listen. In the quiet, in that loud kind of quiet when we feel so alone—he says our name. You'll know it in your spirit. In the watches of the night and in the despair he'll be there. He will always call you by name. That is Jesus. Intimate and personal. He cannot relate to you any other way. He made you. He knows you. He knows your deepest needs better than you do and longs to meet them.

The eyes of God
are never shut . . .

He sees all
Knows all
His presence is with us

Whatever we may walk through
No matter the circumstance.

We are never alone.

Recently I participated in a women's event in Wichita, Kansas. I was thankful to be put on the concierge level at the hotel. On that floor they offer a private room where different meals are served. I enjoy it for the opportunity to get breakfast without even brushing my teeth. I can go in with my hair disheveled and last night's mascara on, grab a cup of coffee and a muffin, and run right back to my room. I was pouring the morning's caffeine boost into a cup when a woman stood right beside me and started to do the same. I quickly glanced at her. Unlike my disheveled self, she had showered and "made up" before entering the world of people. I saw that her eyes looked swollen, but then again I thought it was just the morning puffiness that many of us women know so well. I grunted a little hello.

*"Hi. How ya doin'?"*

*"Ugh. Not so good."*

Her honesty startled me. I have grown accustomed to knowing when the Holy Spirit wants me to pay attention. He is much more about the heart and soul of everyone far more than I can ever be. It registered in my little brain fairly quickly that her eyes had gotten a long dose of tears and the swollenness was much more than what the morning usually offers to a woman.

"What's wrong?"

"Oh, it's just awful. I am so confused. I have been up the whole night. I just don't understand . . ."

She proceeded to tell me that she had met a man over the Internet and they conversed via e-mail for an entire year. He recently invited her to come to town and have dinner with him. He had excused himself to use the restroom and never came back. Just left her sitting there.

My Italian nature can often rage to the surface. It's really the flesh in all of us. I wanted to find the guy and do something drastic. I don't know. Maybe a slow drip on the forehead until he begged for her forgiveness. I just wanted him to pay. Sometimes our first reactions are so Christian, aren't they? I know the Lord just shakes his head waiting for me to get my bearings. Thank God I can usually come to my senses by sensing him and his desires. Praise you Holy Spirit . . . anyway, my heart broke for her, and I knew that Jesus wanted to "love on her" through me. It was a divine appointment.

I turned to her. *"Come sit down on the couch."*

Like a little girl, she obeyed and listened with a child-like heart. I told her about the love of God as she told me how unloved she felt. She had recently moved to get away from an abusive husband as she was trying to make a new life for herself. I desperately wanted her desperately to know that a new life was waiting for her with Jesus. It was as if there was a banner on her forehead that said . . .

*Forgotten, shamed, and lonely.*

What I felt like I was doing the whole time was helping her remove the banner to replace it with his.

*Forgiven, saved, and lovely.*

She had only known the concept of God. She did not know *him*. Her precious soul was dying of thirst, and Jesus longed to quench it. We prayed and I continued to tell her about the love that would never leave her. She invited Jesus in her heart. As we hugged goodbye, under the "puffiness" I saw life come back in her eyes. I left her comforted by the fact that she would finally know true love.

The pain.
Intense.
Excruciating.

As deep as it penetrates—
Jesus' love
Is deeper still.

We are all so thirsty and in need of a touch from God. We go about our busy days trying to maneuver through the unpredictability of life. He longs to meet us. He yearns to let us know that it is safe to be known by him and that as we go through the "busyness," He is aware and offers wholeness and healing. I have found such freedom in the love of God. Before I know it sometimes, I have placed a huge wall in front of my heart. Brick by brick it has slowly been built. Whether it has been sin, shame, or just plain distance from the Lord, the wall is there. I wonder why I feel disconnected. I wonder why I feel empty and alone even in the midst of the noise and the pace of the days. He says…

*Come here. Stop running. Let's talk. I love you.*

What relief. I get to "come clean." I get to unload. I get new perspective. He never leaves in disbelief or anger. I can regain a peace knowing his love doesn't walk away.

A great example of this is the passage in scripture about the woman at the well. To refresh your memory, let's look at it in John 4:5-43 (NIV)

*. . . Jacob's well was there, and Jesus, tired as he was from the journey, sat down by the well. It was about the sixth hour. When a Samaritan woman came to draw water, Jesus said to her,*

*"Will you give me a drink?"*

*(His disciples had gone into the town to buy food.) The Samaritan woman said to him,*

*You are a Jew and I am a Samaritan woman. How can you ask me for a drink?"*

*(for Jews do not associate with Samaritans).*

She was a Samaritan. And what did that mean in those days? They were looked at as "outsiders" and "offensive." The Jews thought they were impure and hated Samaritans. This woman probably went to the well at a time of day where it was "more acceptable" for her presence there. So, picture this . . . here she is alone. It was routine for her. She usually had no one to talk to, especially in a public place. And here is this person. Not just any person. It was Jesus. You could just imagine her keeping her head down. She was probably avoiding eye contact. If she just went about her business maybe he would just go away. But Jesus . . . he isn't going anywhere. And, much to her surprise, Jesus speaks to her. He not only speaks to her but he makes a request.

*"Will you give me a drink?"*

I love this. Here is God—alone with this woman, and he could have said or done all sorts of things. He could have levitated the bucket up from the well. He could have glowed or he could have said like so many eager believers…

*Do you know Jesus as your personal savior?*

No. He made a simple request.

*Give me a drink.*

Was he thirsty? Possibly. But that isn't the point. This is the point.

He wanted to give her something.

She was going to fill her bucket and . . .

Little did she know what this encounter would truly bring. He always wants to give us something. A single encounter with Jesus can change our lives, let alone a diet of his presence.

Aren't we all trying to fill our buckets every day?

*Jesus answered her, "if you knew the gift of God and who it is that asks you for a drink, you would have asked him and he would have given you living water."*

This is so like Jesus. Although he is asking something of her, his true desire is to give her something! She thinks it's the water she is physically drawing, but Jesus knew her need was far greater than her physical thirst. Her soul was dry. Her heart needed his love so desperately. She was lost.

Like the Samaritan woman, Jesus yearns to meet us at the well, when we feel most alone. When we feel most ashamed. The living water that Jesus was talking about was the spring of his unfailing love and his ever-flowing grace. The same is true for each and every one of us. He wants to give us everything we need, which is everything that he is. It is always His heart's desire for us to meet Him at the well.

Let's move on . . .

"Sir," the woman said, "you have nothing to draw with and the well is deep. Where can you get this living water? Are you greater than our father Jacob, who gave us the well and drank from it himself, as did also his sons and his flocks and herds?"

She questions his ability to deliver! I have done that so many times. Haven't you? He saves my life. He rises from the dead. He pledges hundreds of promises that will never be broken. And I either respond defensively or apathetically.

"Lord, I'm not sure that you understand my particular circumstance . . ."

"I'm not sure that you'll come through for me Lord . . ."

"Have you forgotten me?" . . .

Jesus answered, "everyone who drinks this water will be thirsty again, but whoever drinks the water I give him will never thirst. Indeed, the water I give him will become in him a spring of water welling up to eternal life."

But we still yearn we still want...as if he cannot deliver what will ultimately satisfy our souls. His goal is to always offer us life.

*Die and I will give you life.*

*Obey and you will see the glory of the Lord.*

*Give me your heart and I will give you all of myself.*

I love that about God. It is always true. No matter what he asks, his desire is for our good. He wants to give us all that he has and all that He is.

*The woman said to him, "Sir, give me this water so that I won't get thirsty and have to keep coming here to draw water."*

Jesus tells her to go and call her husband, and she informs him that she does not have a husband. Jesus is so gracious to acknowledge her "half-truth." He tells her that what she is saying is accurate, but he gets her to the whole truth.

*"The fact is you have had five husbands, and the man you now have is not your husband."*

I've often tried to rationalize in front of God as if he doesn't see everything. The woman had to be stunned to realize that he not only knew this about her life, but also called her on it as well. Would you have said . . .

"How in the world did you know that? Who are you?"

But as far as I can tell, she responds calmly and tries to change the subject. She tells him,

*"Our fathers worshipped on this mountain and the Jews worship in Jerusalem . . ."*

What????

Can you imagine someone confronting you with the truth and responding with a question something like this...

"So . . . where so you worship?"

Can you relate to the fact that the woman tried to change the subject instead of letting God deal with her heart? We avoid or divert his trying to get to the truth in our souls. Why are we so afraid to be "found out?"

*The road to faithfulness is always through being found out.*

It is so hard to be "found out." But that is where God moves in. He wants to get at the absolute truth in you so that he can give you his absolute truth. Many of us go on for years in denial of the true state of our hearts. We don't grow there. We can actually live somewhat of a slumber. Life passes us by, and we don't experience the fullness of the riches of his love. And we are paralyzed to give it out in return.

What is so wonderful about Jesus in this passage is that He just goes with it and doesn't use the opportunity to shame her. He says,

*"Woman, believe me, a day is coming when you will not worship on this mountain or in Jerusalem but rather with the father."*

We ultimately feel that we will not be met by love. People leave. People laugh. People shame and they gossip. It is failed love. It is conditional love. It is not love at its best. Love at its best is Jesus love. Sacrificial love. Consistent love. Unconditional love. A love that says . . .

*I know you and I love you.*

*Period.*

*Your steadfast love is before my eyes*
*And I walk in faithfulness to you.* PSALM 26:3 NRSV

One of the hardest things is to have the light of an all-knowing God expose our darkest secrets. But even in the midst of her questioning, the woman at the well actually makes the "correct" request without realizing it.

*"Sir, give me this water that I may not thirst . . ."*

Jesus doesn't mind our questions. He doesn't even mind our diversions. He longs for us to be unashamed in his presence, to take him at his word. But we need to make the request. Even in the midst of confusion and pain, we must be willing to look up to Heaven and say,

*"Give me this water that I may not thirst . . ."*

We should enter every day by asking Jesus for the living water. We need it so desperately. What does the phrase, *"give me this water"* look like to you? I know what it looks like for me. And it changes with the seasons of my life.

I may ask for his healing to be poured into a broken heart. I may ask for a gushing river of strength to face a hard situation. I may ask for a river of joy to lift me up when my heart is heavy. I may ask for a sea of peace when I feel stressed out.

As we meet him at the well it is so comforting to know that *his* well never runs dry. And even if it is hard to face our real selves, it is not hard for him. He has seen it long before we have the courage to admit it.

His love beckons our real selves to step forward. Jesus helps us discover our real selves. When we open the doors for the light to come in, the darkness flees. It happened for the woman I met in Wichita. I could see the lies being crushed beneath her feet as the truth of God gave her strength to stand up. She was getting his view of herself and not the view that her emotions were speaking to her. She was finally getting a glimpse of the truth. She was a woman cherished by a living, loving God.

❋ ❋ ❋

The LORD appeared to his people and said,

"I love you people

with a love that will last forever.

That is why I have continued

showing you kindness."

JEREMIAH 31:3 NCV

When our mother died, my sister and I stood on the altar in front of our entire family and friends. What a privilege it was to represent our Lord in front of all of them and at the same time be able to honor our mother's life. We both spoke at the service and I sang a song that I had written. The lyric came to me one evening when my mother was sleeping in her bedroom and I sat at the piano late into the night. Mom had lost so much weight. Her color was so pale and gray, and I knew that she was dying. I remember huddling over those black and white keys, whispering, half-singing as the words came out in prayer as I talked with God.

I FACE THE NIGHT
NOT KNOWING WHAT'S IN SIGHT
OH, PLEASE HOLD ME WHILE I SLEEP
YOU KNOW THESE FEARS RUN DEEP
AND I CAN LOSE MY WAY

I'LL CLING TO YOU
THAT'S ALL I KNOW TO DO
AND KEEP BELIEVING FOR THE BEST
MY HEART CAN FIND ITS REST
IN ALL YOU'VE TOLD ME . . .

I DON'T HAVE TO WISH UPON A STAR
I'LL GO ON BECAUSE OF WHO YOU ARE
I'VE GOT A HOPE AND PRAYER
OH, GOD I KNOW YOU'RE THERE
I GIVE MY EVERY WISH TO YOU
YOU'RE NEVER EVER FAR
MY BRIGHT AND MORNINGSTAR

THE NIGHT IS GONE
MY MIND KEEPS RACING ON
OH I CAN SEE THE MORNING SUN
THE DAY HAS JUST BEGUN
AND I'VE GOT TO LIFT MY HEAD

BUT ONE LOOK AT YOU
AND I CAN SEE THE TRUTH
THAT NOTHING IS IMPOSSIBLE
MY GOD OF MIRACLES
I DO BELIEVE YOU . . .

I DON'T HAVE TO WISH UPON A STAR
I'LL GO ON BECAUSE OF WHO YOU ARE
I'VE GOT A HOPE AND PRAYER
OH, GOD I KNOW YOU'RE THERE
I GIVE MY EVERY WISH TO YOU
YOU'RE NEVER EVER FAR
MY BRIGHT AND MORNINGSTAR

"I'll go on because of who you are..." I sang boldly and passionately before the hundreds of tear-stained faces. What did I have in that moment, if I didn't have him and the hope he brings? I began to read the thoughts that I'd written down the night before, when I couldn't sleep. When I'd finally drifted off that night, my heart was aching, but I knew that I hadn't been abandoned. Jesus was with me.

Remember when the disciples were out at sea?

*That day when evening came, he said to his disciples, "let us go over to the other side." leaving the crowd behind, they took him along, just as he was, in the boat. There were also other boats with him. A furious squall came up, and the waves broke over the boat, so that it was nearly swamped. Jesus was in the stern, sleeping on a cushion. The disciples woke him and said to him, "Teacher, don't you care if we drown?" He got up, rebuked the wind and said to the waves, "Quiet! Be still!" Then the wind died down and it was completely calm. He said to his disciples, "Why are you so afraid? Do you have no faith?" They were terrified and asked each other, "Who is this? Even the wind and the waves obey him!"*

MARK 4:35-41 NIV

*"Don't you care?"*

I have asked the Lord that question many times throughout my relationship with him. Especially through the pain of "losing" a loved one. All sorts of waves of emotions have flooded over me and I have felt like I was going under. Surely I could take no more. Then somehow with the dawn of a new day I see his leading and I sense his love. The winds die down, and I am in awe of the calm I experience.

Give thanks to the LORD because he is good.

His love continues forever.

Give thanks to the God of gods.

His love continues forever.

Give thanks to the Lord of lords.

His love continues forever.

Only he can do great miracles.

His love continues forever.

With his wisdom he made the skies.

His love continues forever.

He spread out the earth on the seas.

His love continues forever.

He made the sun and the moon.

His love continues forever.

He made the sun to rule the day.

His love continues forever.

He made the moon and stars to rule the night.

His love continues forever. . . .

He remembered us when we were in trouble.

His love continues forever.

He freed us from our enemies.

His love continues forever.

He gives food to every living creature.

His love continues forever.

Give thanks to the God of heaven.

His love continues forever.

PSALM 136:1-9, 23-26 NCV

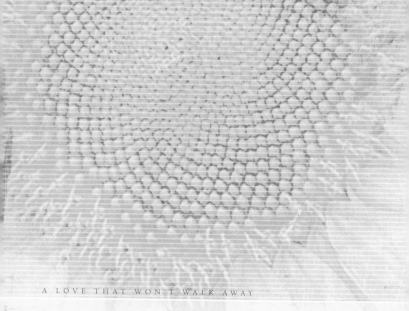

## A LOVE THAT WON'T WALK AWAY

Some days are easier than others cause life's not tac
Some days you hide under the covers till the storm clouds b
You feel like your faith is dying, but please don't gi

Cause that's just how it goes how life turns, how it rolls, through the fire and through
It may hurt, it may bruise, it may leave you confused, but you wil
cause His kind of love is a love that won't w

So don't let the rain take you
Don't let the wind beat
Don't let the waves crash against you and turn your hea
cause God is right there beside you and He wants you

Oh, that's just h
How life turns, how it rolls, through the fire and through
It may hurt, it may bruise, it may leave you confused, but you wil
cause His kind of love is a love that won't w

86    KATHY TROCCOLI

OUR PEACE IS
*to Live in God's Love*

I often say that one of the many things I love about Jesus is that he is a keeper of his word. From the first day that I met him, he told me there would be sorrow and tears and tribulation. But he also told me that he would be with me through it all, carrying me . . . comforting me . . . walking me into the future. He desired my trust—and he would take care of the rest.

John 3:30 says . . .

*He must increase, but I must decrease.*

Growing closer with Jesus is a process and a continually "growing and knowing" time. We don't say "I do" and even come close to knowing our mates as well as we do two years later, five years later, or thirty years later. We don't strike up an acquaintance one day and know the deepest heart of that friend in one week. And the knowing and growing—the trust—it takes time together. It takes communication. It takes striving to know the heart of that person. It is a commitment and investment. It is the same with Jesus. So we can quickly see the truth of this verse.

He must keep increasing, and I must keep decreasing. It is not in decreasing our view of ourselves, but increasing our view of God. Increasing our understanding of him and his perspective on things. Some people are known to be so "full of themselves." It is usually associated with arrogance. But we can be full of ourselves in many other ways. It can be anger or guilt or fear. It can be insecurity or shame. In either case, there is no room for Jesus to live. Your identity and your view of love are wrapped up in your brokenness.

You're nothing? No! You're something. He told you you're valuable by offering his very life. We have trouble believing that we are really loved—especially in our failings, in our sin, and in our shame.

days you hide under the covers till the storm clouds blow away

feel like your faith is dying, but please don't give up yet

'cause that's just how it goes, how life turns, how it rolls, through the fire and through the pain

my hurt, it may bruise, it may leave you confused, but you will be okay

'cause His kind of love is a love that won't walk away

don't let the rain take your courage

don't let the wind beat you down

don't let the waves crash against you

'cause God is right there beside you

that's just how it goes

life turns, how it rolls, through the

my hurt, it may bruise, it may leave you confused, but you'll be okay

'cause His kind of love is a love that

Let me hear what God the LORD will speak,

    for he will speak peace to his people,

    to his faithful, to those who turn to him in their hearts.

Surely his salvation is at hand for those who fear him,

    that his glory may dwell in our land.

Steadfast love and faithfulness will meet;

    righteousness and peace will kiss each other.

Faithfulness will spring up from the ground,

    and righteousness will look down from the sky.

The LORD will give what is good,

    and our land will yield its increase.

    Righteousness will go before him,

    and will make a path for his steps.

PSALM 85:8-13 NRSV

I have a few favorite stories in the scriptures. Some of you who have read my writings or have heard me speak know that I could go on for days about Mary at the feet of Jesus.

I could talk for hours about the hope that was offered to us on that blessed resurrection day.

I could sing forever about the love that was given on the cross.

But one of the places in the scriptures that I will often go back to is where Jesus conveys a message to Peter after the resurrection. It has reminded me over and over again of the tender loving heart of God. I pray it will remind you also. Let's go back to the last supper in Mark 14:28-31 (NIV). Jesus said . . .

*But after I have risen, I will go ahead of you into Galilee.*
And Peter declared . . .
*"Even if all fall away, I will not."*

I could just picture Peter not even giving Jesus time to finish his sentence. He was so certain of his commitment and love and friendship. And I am sure that he truly meant it. Isn't it remarkable how many of us have said Peter's words with the same conviction? Maybe we have been the ones who've been made such a promise. The human blood that runs though our veins also makes us susceptible to a human and conditional love.

*"I tell you the truth," Jesus answered, "Today—yes, tonight—before the rooster crows twice you yourself will disown me three times."*

Peter wouldn't hear of it. He insisted emphatically, *"Even if I have to die with you, I will never disown you," and all the others said the same.*

It's what I like to term "forever talk."

I will love you forever.

I will never leave you.

You don't have to worry about that with me.

Many times the last sentence in this famous passage of scripture is ignored.

*And all the others said the same.*

They all proclaimed their loyalty. They all dodged their promises.

When the soldiers came and arrested him the scriptures say,

*Then everyone deserted him and fled.* MARK 14:50 (NIV)

We have all had our hearts broken, but we also have all broken our promises. You know why? It is because *we* are broken. The good news is that Jesus never breaks a vow. When He says,

"Even if everyone leaves you I will not," it will be for eternity. When he says, "Even if I have to die with you I will not disown you," He did die for you so that you would have His love forever.

Peter was so passionate in his words of undying commitment to Jesus. Now here he is just hours from those bold promises of devotion.

*"I don't know this man."* MARK 14:71 (NIV)

The scriptures say that he broke down and wept when the rooster crowed. God kept his word and Peter surely did not. He was utterly devastated about his quick about-face when people started to associate him with the Lord. Peter saw the dishonesty and cowardliness immediately. But the deep anguish in his soul was met by a supernatural touch three days later. God sees the darkest parts of our being and brings the light of his love to every corner.

My very first song on the radio was called "Stubborn Love." I still sing it from time to time.

They refused to listen;

    they forgot the miracles you did for them.

So they became stubborn and turned against you,

    choosing a leader to take them back to slavery.

But you are a forgiving God.

    You are kind and full of mercy.

You do not become angry quickly,

    and you have great love.

So you did not leave them.

NEHEMIAH 9:17 NCV

It's your stubborn love

That never lets go of me

I don't understand how you can stay

Perfect love embracing the worst in me

How I long for your stubborn love

His perfect love embraces the very worst in us. There is no other love like that! It is so hard for us to fathom that kind of love. But it is true. It is only Jesus love.

After the burial of Jesus, Mary Magdalene, Mary the mother of James, and Salome brought spices to the tomb. They wanted to anoint the body of Jesus, *"But when they looked up, they saw that the stone, which was very large, had been rolled away. As they entered the tomb, they saw a young man dressed in a white robe sitting on the right side, and they were alarmed."* MARK 16:4, 5 (NIV)

Here is the best part of the whole Peter story. I want to cry every time I read it. The Lord is so intimate and so precious to call us to Himself and to call us by name.

*"Don't be alarmed,"* he said. *"You are looking for Jesus the Nazarene, who was crucified. He has risen! He is not here. See the place where they laid him, but go, tell his disciples and Peter, 'he is going ahead of you into Galilee. There you will see him, just as he told you.'"* MARK 16:6, 7 (NIV)

*"I will not remove from [you]*
*my steadfast love,*
*or be false to my faithfulness."*

PSALM 89:33 NRSV

some days are easier than others cause life's not tailor made

some days you hide under the covers till the storm clouds blow away

you feel like your faith is dying, but please don't give up yet

cause thats just how it goes how life turns, how it rolls

through the fire and through the pain,

it may hurt, it may bruise, it may leave you scarred, but you will be okay

cause His hand of love is a love that won't walk away

and don't let the rain take your courage,

don't let the wind knock you down,

don't let the waves rough against you and turn your head around,

cause God is right there beside you as you make it through,

cause thats just how it

how life turns, how it rolls,

it may hurt, it may bruise, it may leave you scarred,

cause His hand of love is a love that won't walk away

"GO TELL HIS DISCIPLES AND PETER."

When I first read this, I didn't read it like I do now. As I have grown in my understanding of Jesus and have seen my own depravity, I read it with a different heart. It is a heart of humility and gratefulness. I know what I am capable of apart from the grace of God. He is so merciful. The Lord knew the hopelessness and loneliness that Peter must have been feeling. Can you imagine when the women got back and delivered the message? The Lord had risen from the dead. What a miracle! What good news for the men he had called his friends! It was all about to make sense. In the euphoria of it all, could you just see Peter?

He mentioned *me*?

He said *my* name?

I can picture them shaking him.

*"Peter. Listen. Jesus rose from the dead!"*

*"I know. I know! But he really mentioned me?"*

The amazing love of God. It is not only a love that doesn't walk away, it walks towards us when we need it the most.

Guilt.

Regret.

Anger.

They loom over your sky.

Thick and ominous.

     Exploding with a storm so fierce—

Your vision is blinded.

Your hope is washed away.

Condemnation floods the banks

Of your heart and mind.


    Look up.

    Look up.


      The sun breaks through the sky

      With rays of mercy,

      forgiveness and hope

      You can bask in his love.

So many of us live in and out of seasons of relationships. We might just say "I haven't seen her in years" or "I lost track of him years ago." It can be the same with Jesus. We might say the same of him or believe that he has said the same about us.

*Surely he has forgotten me.*

Sometimes we get bitter because we have forgotten all the things he has told us about himself . . . or we refuse to see where he has been faithful. When we are in darkness, we must remember what he revealed in the light. He is faithful. He is just. He is merciful. He is trustworthy.

David prays a beautiful prayer in Psalm 57 . . .

*Have mercy on me, O God.*
*Have mercy on me,*
*For in you my soul takes refuge.*

*I will take refuge in the*
*Shadow of your wings*
*Until the disaster has passed.*

*I cry out to God most high,*
*To God, who fulfills his purpose for me.*
*He sends from Heaven and saves me . . .*
*God sends his love and his faithfulness.*

PSALM 57:1-3 (NIV)

*He sends from Heaven . . .*

God sends everything he is. It is all wrapped up in his love as he fulfills his purpose for you. You must not forget. You must choose to remember who he is. We must launch our hearts into the Heavenlies. That is where we will always gain revelation about God's love and faithfulness. And that is where once again we gain revelation of our worth to him. When we focus on those truths, we can live with a holy confidence that the God of the universe cherishes us.

Since the day I began my relationship with Jesus in 1978, I have gotten to know him in ways that I never imagined I would. Similar to a marriage, I have grown to trust him, lean on him—believe him when he tells me something.

The scriptures say that those who look to him are radiant and their faces are never covered with shame. Why? Confidence. A certainty. Look at the spirit of a child who knows that their parent adores them. Look at the countenance of a woman who has been honored by her husband year after year.

God's love enhances our beauty. God's love enhances our hope. His love calls us to our real selves and calls us to life.

We have all benefited from the rich blessings he brought to us—one gracious blessing after another. For the law was given through Moses; God's unfailing love and faithfulness came through Jesus Christ.

JOHN 1:16-17 NLT

A few final examples . . .

I was in the Nashville airport recently. I was waiting for my luggage at baggage claim. It was a late flight, so everyone looked kind of disheveled and tired. I looked up and saw the most delightful scene. A little girl was dancing—and dancing as if no one was watching. Sweet twirls and ballet steps. People around the carousel looked up and glanced at her. Some smiled. I stared at her the whole time.

As I watched her pirouettes and leaps, I was jealous of the fact that she could live so freely in the presence of others. In my mind, I pictured myself doing the same thing. I would be considered unstable or insane and whisked off by airport security. There have been times in my life when I was so aware of God's love for me that I wanted to shout it out my car window. I wanted to yell it from the roof of my house. I wanted to dance around in an airport . . .

When any of us truly grasp the love of God, it is a glorious revelation. I can still weep at communion when the words "Do this in remembrance of me" are quoted. I am giddy some days at the thought that he has been my provision when I had no one to provide for me. He has surrounded me with people that love me and know me. I have neither been left nor forgotten.

I must say I have not always been conscious of his presence. I have worried and succumbed to deep anguish and loss of sleep. But as I get older and find that change always occurs and that pain will show its ugly head through the course of every life, I have a sense that "all will be well." I have grown in confidence that he will not leave and that his plan unfolds so much more beautifully than I could ever have orchestrated.

Have you ever wondered why some people seem to handle tragedy and loss so much better than others or, if you're honest, so much easier than you? Why is that? Is it just a personality style? *God made her that way but not me?* I've done enough thinking and praying on this issue to tell you my heartfelt belief. It has little to do with personality and everything to do with proper relationship and eternal perspective. It is a supernatural confidence that God gives to our fragile human hearts. It is a "knowing" that God is a keeper of his word and that nothing is ever as it seems.

I meet thousands of women all year long. Some of my favorite moments at a conference are when I get to meet women of all ages at a signing table. If time allows I will attempt to greet every last person in the line. It is important to me to hear their "stories." So often I welcome it because it ignites my faith. With the comfort women receive from God, they in turn will comfort me. I am told I do that from the platform, but I feel like it is a "give and take" for the audience and me. We are all in the same ship sailing toward Heaven's shores. It is one of the many ways that God has set up the body of Christ to be able to encourage one another. We see and hear about his faithfulness, provision, and healing, and it lifts our faith.

There is such a vast difference between the women who have put their confidence in Christ and those who are "heavy-laden." It is truly remarkable to me. It is the difference between the beauty of a little girl dancing freely and a little girl cowering in a corner. So many women wear scarves or knitted caps on their heads or are just plain bald from the ravages of breast cancer, yet they possess a radiance that I envy. Some of them may be at the last days of their lives, but they have come to laugh with their friends and hear about the goodness of God. One woman recently was waiting in line. I was aware of her because of her frailty. I was anxious to meet her. I am always in awe of the sick who get out to an event without worrying about their condition. (I've watched cancer be a death sentence in my family. People were confined to beds and couches in hospitals and homes.) It was her turn in line. She was frail and her skin tone had that familiar yellow hue. Her fingers were delicately thin—almost skeletal. I got up and wrapped my arms around her.

*How are you doing?*

She answered slowly and with a smile. It was as if each word was ringing throughout the Heavens. A weak woman on earth giving glory to her powerful God in the Heavens. I could almost sense the angelic host listening in . . .

*I can actually feel his hand on my shoulder.*

*Cancer has changed my life for the good.*

*I can't put my hopes on living. But I will put my hope in him.*

She reached for me—wiping the tears from *my* eyes. I saw the Lord so clearly in her person. I asked her if I could pray for her. How gracious she was. I knew that many must have prayed over her, but she welcomed it so humbly. I knew that she wanted anything that God wanted for her. She was a woman who was able to see him in the moments. As we both said "amen," I couldn't help but see in her the beauty of a bride in love. She possessed a quiet confidence in the One who pledged his love to her two thousand years ago. Her confidence and peace were arresting. I fell more in love with Jesus that day. As she walked away, I yearned for her to live, but then realized that she *was* truly living more fully than most healthy people I know. One thing was true. We will both dance freely before the throne of God someday.

He is so close to the brokenhearted.

He is so near

to the weary soul.

He is so present

in our suffering.

He never hides his face

But offers a hiding place.

Allow yourself to fall.

He's waiting to catch you.

Every single one of us goes to bed each night with dreams, plans, and desires. In our minds, all the street-lights are green. Each of us wakes up every day without knowing what the next twenty-four hours will bring. Everything we held in our hearts the night before may meet up with a red stoplight at every juncture. Even if we are walking through a "sweet" season, a challenging one may be just ahead. It is because we are living under the sun and the moon. It is because blood pours through our hearts every day. It is because sin entered the world. We are not in Heaven. With all the uncertainty in life one thing is certain: The love of Jesus Christ is unchanging. It will never walk away. ✻

CAUSE THAT'S JUST HOW IT GOES

HOW LIFE TURNS HOW IT ROLLS

THROUGH THE FIRE AND THROUGH THE PAIN

IT MAY HURT IT MAY BRUISE

IT MAY LEAVE YOU CONFUSED

BUT YOU WILL BE OKAY

CAUSE HIS KIND OF LOVE IS A LOVE

THAT WON'T WALK AWAY

**KATHY TROCCOLI** is an award-winning singer, author and speaker who has sold more than 1.5 million albums, garnered numerous number 1 radio hits, received two Dove Awards and a Grammy® nomination with her rich, melodic voice. Whether singing or speaking, Kathy is driven by a passionate desire to share Christ and the hope that comes from knowing Him. She is the author of several books and Bible studies and is a sought-after conference speaker. In 2003, Kathy was selected by the readers of *Today's Christian Woman* magazine as one of the four most influential women in America. Among her other books are *Hope for a Woman's Heart*, *Am I Not Still God*, and the Bible study series that includes *Falling in Love with Jesus*, *Living in Love with Jesus*, and *Forever in Love with Jesus*.

For more information, please visit troccoli.com.

The LORD still waits for you

    to come to him so he can

    show you his love and compassion.

For the LORD is a faithful God.

Blessed are those who wait for him to help them.

ISAIAH 30:18 NLT